Dear Jeanine.
He who began a
You will bring it
P.h.

DEVELOPING A SOUND CHRISTIAN CHARACTER

PRINCIPLES OF CHARACTER DEVELOPMENT FOR EVERY BELIEVER

FOREWORD BY
DR. SOLA FOLA-ALADE

PETER BASHORUN

DEVELOPING A SOUND CHRISTIAN CHARACTER
Copyright 2011 © Peter Bashorun

ISBN:978-0-9564767-8-4

Published by Vision Media Comm.
Email: info@colourdesigns.co.uk
Tel: +44 7903 822 987

Printed in United Kingdom

ACKNOWLEDGEMENTS

I give praise to the Almighty God and thank Him for not only saving me, but also choosing and using me in this generation.

I say thank you to all the members of RCCG Renewal Ground. You respond positively to God's words of Renewal through His servant.

I also say thank you to Pastor (Mrs.) Janet Adedipe of RCCG Redemption Parish London, UK for releasing me by the power of God into the ministry and my destiny.

And to my writing consultant Lekan Opasina, God has used you to support and encourage me to put my thoughts in a way that is readable. And also Oladapo Awosokanre for proof-reading and editing this book.

A big thank you to my lovely wife Regina and children Tosin, Tope, Tobi, and Tolu for releasing me and supporting me to do what God has called me to do.

DEDICATION

I dedicate this book to my LORD Jesus Christ, the Way, the Truth and Life, KING of kings and the LORD of lords with whom there is no variableness. And to every believer that wants to live a Principled Renewed life.

FOREWORD

In the time I have known Pastor Peter, he has always demonstrated exemplary Christian character which is evident in his ministry, family & personal life. The title & ethos of this book therefore aligns with his person.

Character is an attribute that should distinguish us as Christians; our character should show forth in all facets of life & spheres of society. Character is what sustains leaders and gives them the impetus to successfully rule over what God has commissioned them to bring to pass on earth.

If character is of utmost importance in accomplishing destiny, it's imperative that it is developed in all of us. In this book, Pastor Peter has expounded on a number of components that form our character. He has used biblical insight to determine how as individuals, we can renew each of these components.

The first chapter deals with the make up of an unblemished character after which, each chapter deals extensively with the renewal of an essential component of our character from renewing our hearts, minds, thoughts, conscience and tongue. It moves on to deal with renewing our walk, vision, temple and love. It concludes by dealing with how we build with character and how the renewed character of a believer should stand out.

Scripture determines in Hebrews 13:5 that if our character is sound, God will not in anyway fail us, nor let us down:
5 *Let your* **character** *or moral disposition be free from love of money [including greed, avarice, lust, and craving for earthly possessions] and be satisfied with your present [circumstances and with what you have]; for He [God] Himself has said, I will not in any way fail you nor give you up nor leave you without support. [I will] not, not in any degree leave you helpless nor forsake nor let [you] down (relax My hold on you)! [Assuredly not!]*- **Hebrews 13:5 Amplified.**

This book is a must read for anyone that wants to develop an impeccable character that will enable them develop fruit that lasts. I recommend it to all.

Dr. Sola Fola-Alade

TABLE OF CONTENTS

INTRODUCTION

RUTH 3:11 says, "and now, my daughter, don't be afraid. I will do for you all you ask. All my fellow townsmen know that you are a woman of noble character."

Character is the quality that makes a person or group of people different from others. It can also be a person's moral nature, strength, a noticeable person and a testimonial. Another word for character is nature, attributes, disposition, make-up, marked traits, personality and temperament. The moment someone repents of his or her sins and surrenders to Christ, he or she will be translated from the kingdom of darkness to the kingdom of God; and so such a one is expected to conduct himself or herself as a kingdom citizen. As believers, it is our responsibility with the help of God to develop a sound (solid, undamaged, well-constructed, firm, perfect, complete, tried and true, trustworthy etc) character which will differentiate us from all others.

Character is not what you can exhibit once in a while or latent potential, but it is the totality of your behaviour, the way and motive of your heart. **Psalm 17:3 says, "Though you probe my heart and examine me at night, though you test me, you will find nothing; I have resolved that my mouth will not sin."** You see, character is not only the visible but the invisible part of your life that is known by only you and God.

Character is the ability to minimise or eliminate the guidance of the flesh over our life and be guided by the spirit. And if I may add, character is more important than success and endures longer than popularity. I strongly believe that character is better than good name, because as soon as your character betrays you, your good name is over. Your character will speak for or against you when you are alive and after you have gone. That is why as a person, I have always been very careful the way I behave, conduct myself, act, or interact with anyone that comes my way both for believers and non believers.

> CHARACTER IS NOT WHAT YOU CAN EXHIBIT ONCE IN A WHILE OR LATENT POTENTIAL, BUT IT IS THE TOTALITY OF YOUR BEHAVIOUR, THE WAY AND MOTIVE OF YOUR HEART.

Character makes Ruth to be different from Orpah in the Bible; she was a woman of noble character, strength, worth, bravery and capability. Ruth had an exemplary virtue that others could see and know, she was unswerving and had a selfless devotion to desolate Naomi. Her character made her steady in standing by Naomi which brought a positive consequence her way, however, Orpah's attitude brought her negative consequences and she was forgotten right from Ruth chapter one.

Character will exalt both men and women to the company of the wisest and the best. Character is not what you have, like money, career, properties etc, but who you are. You can have money and not be a trustworthy person. Character is like a smoke, in as much as you cannot hide a smoke, so also you cannot hide your character, sooner or later it will eventually expose you and show who you are.

Character can either be positive or negative, but I implore you as believers to develop a sound Christian character, Ruth a Moabitess, was a poor woman; though poverty often obscures virtue, yet Ruth's virtue was taken notice of and could not be hidden, her virtues took away the reproach of her poverty. Ruth had been remarkable for humility, which paved the way to this honour. The less she proclaimed her own goodness, the more her neighbours took notice of her. It is only when our behaviours (as believers and unbelievers) are governed by principles and we live in harmony with them that we can experience positive outcomes as in the case of Ruth.

I believe that God has called believers to live a life that pleases Him. The fruits of our salvation must be evident for all to see. As you read this book, you would be able to understand what it means to live a Renewed Life. In this book you will be able to learn the principles of character development in a believers life.

BILLY GRAHAM ONCE SAID, "INTEGRITY IS THE GLUE THAT HOLDS OUR WAY OF LIFE TOGETHER. WE MUST CONSTANTLY STRIVE TO KEEP OUR INTEGRITY INTACT. WHEN WEALTH IS LOST, NOTHING IS LOST; WHEN HEALTH IS LOST, SOMETHING IS LOST; WHEN CHARACTER IS LOST, ALL IS LOST."

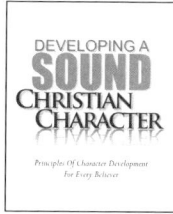

DEVELOPING A
SOUND
CHRISTIAN
CHARACTER

*Principles Of Character Development
For Every Believer*

CHAPTER 1

UNDAMAGED CHARACTER – WHAT DOES IT INVOLVE?

"Now this is our boast: Our conscience testifies that we have conducted ourselves in the world, and especially in our relations with you, in the holiness and sincerity that are from God. We have done so not according to worldly wisdom but according to God's grace."
2 CORINTHIANS 1:12

As Kingdom citizens, developing a sound and undamaged character involves sincerity, because we are the mirror that the unbelievers look at and it really shows who we are.

Self Conduct

The way and manner you conduct yourself is very important, you should deal and relate with people of all sorts with sincerity. There should not be any double dealings as Christians. If you want to be treated well, treat others well; the way you behave and your attitude towards others speaks volumes about you. Emerson put character this way, "What you are shouts so loudly in my ears, I cannot hear what you say." Paul in defending his trustworthiness against the slanders and rumours being spread about him, appeals to the witness of his own conscience and to the Corinthians' firsthand knowledge of his character. Paul had spent 18 months with them when he first came to Corinth **(Acts 18:11),** he stayed for a year and a half, teaching them the word of God, so they were not ignorance of his integrity.

For you to have an undamaged character, you have to be a person of principles and a true child of God, as it is possible to be a Christian and lack principles. As a man or woman of plain dealing; people should know how to place you, your yes should be yes and your no to be no. An undamaged character involves a believer who is not a man or woman who pretends to be one thing and is another thing entirely, but a man or woman of sincerity. Some people are as cool as cucumber when they are in the church, but they are like a wolf outside the church, this should not be; our lives should be an example for others and bring glory to God.

AS A MAN OR WOMAN OF PLAIN DEALING; PEOPLE SHOULD KNOW HOW TO PLACE YOU, YOUR YES SHOULD BE YES AND YOUR NO TO BE NO.

Ambassador Paul and his fellow workers acted and conducted themselves well not only among the Corinthians but also in the world. They conducted themselves in holiness and sincerity that are from God and not according to the worldly wisdom; it was according to the grace of God. However, these things just don't happen, it starts first with self, (this I call inside out), it starts with who you are and your motives.

You have to improve yourself before improving your relationship with others and you have to be trustworthy to be trusted. You've got to conduct yourself in such a way that it would bring glory to God with pure motives and Godly sincerity, and not make giving gifts an excuse for not wanting to serve and give your life to God. For you to possess an undamaged character, you must have principles (deep fundamental truths and ethics) and values that you live by. Your values would dictate your character, so you've got to build on good values that will dictate your character and behaviour.

If one of your values is love or integrity, you would live by it in demonstrating practical love in every circumstance. **Matthew 5:44 says, "But I tell you: Love your enemies and pray for those who persecute you."** You need to be a man or woman of principles to love your enemies and not want to retaliate for any ill or evil done to you. And if it is integrity, you must hold on to it to be a man or woman of character. So now you understand that good character is the direct opposite to bad ones. The life and behaviour of citizens in the kingdom of God is opposite to the kind of life in the world. Even some of the people of the world live by principles, because principles are fundamental truths that have universal application. We are ambassadors of Christ, we represent the Kingdom of Heaven and so our character must reflect that.

YOU HAVE TO IMPROVE YOURSELF BEFORE IMPROVING YOUR RELATIONSHIP WITH OTHERS AND YOU HAVE TO BE TRUSTWORTHY TO BE TRUSTED.

WALK BLAMELESS

"LORD, who may dwell in your sanctuary? Who may live on your holy hill? He whose walk is blameless and who does what is righteous, who speaks the truth from his heart." – PSALM 15:1-2.

Many Christians believe God for miracles, signs and wonders but do not intend to live a blameless life. Many believe God for breakthroughs, but do not live a holy life. To dwell in His sanctuary and enter into His presence, you will need to lead a blameless life, do what is right and speak the truth from your heart. In your dealings with people, you need to be what you really profess to be, sound at heart, approving yourself to God, be in integrity in all that you do; your conversation and endeavours should stand complete in the will of God.

I know for sure that there will be mistakes as we journey here on earth, but according to Stephen Covey author of 'The 7 Habits of Highly Effective People', he said, "Not to acknowledge a mistake, not to correct it and learn from it, is a mistake of a different order". He further stated that this second mistake, this cover-up, empowers the first, giving it disproportionate importance, and causes far deeper injury to self. We need to correct mistakes and work towards perfection.

Undamaged character involves being honest and just in all your dealings. It is God's will for us to live an undamaged Christian life, not only for us because of the future, but to show and prove that we are indeed children of God and heirs of the Kingdom.

TO DWELL IN HIS SANCTUARY AND ENTER INTO HIS PRESENCE, YOU WILL NEED TO LEAD A BLAMELESS LIFE, DO WHAT IS RIGHT AND SPEAK THE TRUTH FROM YOUR HEART.

INTEGRITY

Integrity is one of the values that is lacking in Christendom today and you cannot develop an undamaged character without being a man or woman of integrity. As Christians, we are not expected to live a corrupt life or a life of double standards, we are supposed to set a good example for others by living a whole and sound life. Integrity is so important at the church that I pastor that we have it in the values that descrive us.

"The integrity of the upright guides them, but the unfaithful are destroyed by their duplicity." - Proverbs 11:3

The integrity of the upright guides and lead them like Joseph in **Genesis 39:7-12** who refused to sin against God by sleeping with his master's wife. Joseph refused to go to bed with her and also refused to sin against God though no one was there to see him, *v9 ... How then could I do such a wicked thing and sin against God?* He was then unjustly thrown into prison, his only crime being his attractiveness and moral integrity. Integrity will make you to stand out among others, it is in you wherever you may be or go. The unfaithful are destroyed by their duplicity (dishonesty, false ways) and by their lack of integrity.

Righteousness guards the man of integrity, but wickedness overthrows the sinner. – Proverbs 13:6. Righteousness will guard (shield, supervise, secure, protect) and keep a man or woman of integrity in their ways. Godliness will guard the path of the blameless and he or she will be secured from ruin. Undamaged character involves honesty in all your actions, adhering conscientiously to the sacred and eternal rules of equity and dealing sincerely with both God and man. Your integrity will keep you from the temptations of Satan, which will not prevail over you. Please note that being tempted is not a sin, it is when one yields to temptation that one sins.

The wickedness of the sinners will overthrow them eventually, it is their own wickedness that corrects and destroys them. So make up your mind to live a life of integrity, hold on onto it and don't compromise your standard.

PRAYER

Father, help me to live an undamaged Christian life in my conduct as well as my dealings with God and man. Help me to be guarded by integrity in Jesus' mighty name.

INTEGRITY WILL MAKE YOU TO STAND OUT AMONG OTHERS, IT IS IN YOU WHEREVER YOU MAY BE OR GO.

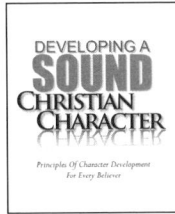

DEVELOPING A
SOUND
CHRISTIAN
CHARACTER

*Principles Of Character Development
For Every Believer*

CHAPTER 2

THE RENEWED HEART

*"Above all else, guard your heart,
for it is the wellspring of life."*
PROVERBS 4:23

The heart is the centre of a person's emotions, affections or innermost thoughts. This is where the deepest and sincerest feelings are located and in it lays our passion and enthusiasm for life. The heart being the core of inner self is the center of a person's being and intellect. It is with the heart that a person feels, perceives and makes moral choices, that is why it is very important for your heart to be renewed. It is also with the heart that one seeks and responds to God. The heart can be a storage, that is why the Bible says in **Matthew 12:34, For out of the overflow of the heart the mouth speaks.** You speak out of what you have stored in your heart. Whatever you store in your heart, you will act and speaks with your mouth

THE SPRING OF LIFE

Your heart needs to be worked on and be renewed, because it affects every other thing that you do, it has to be kept pure for out of it are the important things of life. The truth is that the goodness of your words and actions is traceable to the good things you store up in your heart. The heart is the originator and the source of every important thing in life. When someone has joy or sorrow in their heart, because the heart is the seat of emotions, it will show for others to see by the attitude that they put up.

Our heart is like an inside-out system, whatever is in our heart is displayed and exhibited by our attitude and then your attitude dictates your actions and reactions to issues. **Isaiah 65:14 says, "My servants will sing out of the joy of their hearts, but you will cry out from anguish of heart and wail in brokenness of spirit."** So it is when joy is stored in your heart that you can sing and rejoice, the same applies when there is fear in the heart.

Psalms 143:4 says, "My heart, within me is dismayed or when there is hatred in the heart, **Leviticus 19:17 says, "Do not hate your brother in your heart."** And it can be the seat of love.

1 Timothy 1:5 says, "The goal of this command is love, which comes from a pure heart." The reason why you should guard your heart is because you can store in it many things either good or bad. It is then important that you have to keep and guard your heart with all vigilance for out of it flows the springs of life. For the heart to be renewed it has to be circumcised.

A CIRCUMCISED HEART

Your heart will need to be circumcised so as to be renewed and for you to develop a sound Christian character, because life depends on it. The foreskin of your heart has to be circumcised before it can be renewed. Why do you need your heart to be circumcised or surgically operated upon when you are already a Christian? It is because the Bible says in **Jeremiah 17:9 (Amp)** **"The heart is deceitful above all things, and it is exceedingly perverse and corrupt and severely, mortally sick! Who can know it [perceive, understand, be acquainted with his own heart and mind]"**.

This is one of the reasons why you should allow God to circumcise your heart, the "wellspring of life", in which wickedness must not be allowed to take root. The heart is deceitful above all things, it is exceedingly perverse, wicked, corrupt and severely, mortally sick; no human being can know or understand your heart or what is going on unless you say or act in a way that shows the state of your heart. Oh! I can see you and even be talking to you without knowing your heart; it is true who can understand it! For your heart to be renewed, it has to be circumcised, so it can be free and purged from every deceit, wickedness, corruption and be cured by God.

THE FORESKIN OF YOUR HEART HAS TO BE CIRCUMCISED BEFORE IT CAN BE RENEWED.

Another reason why you need circumcision (surgical operation) is in **Ezekiel 11:19 (Amp)** **"And I will give them one heart [a new heart] and I will put a new spirit within them, and I will take the stony [unnaturally hardened] heart out of their flesh,**

and will give them a heart of flesh [sensitive and responsive to the touch of their God]."

It is only God that can perform this operation in you; He will give you a new heart, an undivided heart to replace the unnaturally wicked, corrupt and hardened heart. Why does God need to give you a new heart? So that you can be sensitive and responsive to the touch of God and have a good character as a Christian, undivided heart, new spirit, an inner spiritual and moral transformation that results in single-minded commitment to the LORD and to His will.

For you to develop a sound Christian character, you've got to believe God for renewal of your heart, let Him remove the stony and stubborn heart and give you a heart of flesh that will be sensitive and responsive to the touch of God. The LORD wants to recapture your heart and lay hold on it, are you going to let Him?

Ezekiel 14:5 I will do this to recapture the hearts of the people of Israel, who have all deserted me for their idols. When your heart is recaptured by God, you will have joy to serve, joy will replace sorrow, love will replace hatred, boldness will replace fear and trust will replace doubt.

Ecclesiastes 10:2 says, "The heart of the wise inclines to the right, but the heart of the fool to the left." Naturally, we know that the heart is positioned on the left hand side of the chest, but after the heavenly surgical operation the heart moves to the right and you can now see things from the Kingdom perspective and not with the worldly perspective. From then on, the renewed heart (the wise) will begin to choose and follow the right path.

PRAYER

LORD I pray in the name of Jesus, that you will recapture my heart, circumcise it and renew it. Where there has been hatred, bring love, where there has been sorrow, bring joy, where there has been fear, bring boldness and where there has been doubt, bring trust. Thank you because you have answered in Jesus' mighty name.

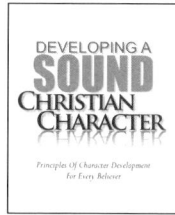

DEVELOPING A
SOUND
CHRISTIAN
CHARACTER

*Principles Of Character Development
For Every Believer*

CHAPTER 3

THE RENEWED MIND

"Therefore, I urge you, brothers, in view of God's mercy, to offer your bodies as living sacrifices, holy and pleasing to God-this is your spiritual act of worship. Do not conform any longer to the pattern of this world, but be transformed by the renewing of your mind. Then you will be able to test and approve what God's will is-his good, pleasing and perfect will." – ROMANS 12:1-2.

The mind is the acting or ruling part of us, the centre for affections and is equivalent with the heart therefore the desires of a man are the desires of his mind. It is the ability to be aware of things, to think and reason, originating in the brain. It is also a way of thinking and feeling: somebody's emotional and moral nature, where the most private thoughts and feelings are hidden. It is a battle ground where the devil and his demons fight for supremacy, if he can win the battle in the mind, he has captured the fellow.

TRANSFORMATION

Believers are to offer their bodies as living sacrifices, in contrast to dead animal sacrifices. ("living" in the sense of having the new life of the Holy Spirit). Your spiritual act must not be merely ritual activity but the involvement of heart, mind and soul. Transformation takes place as a result of the renewing of your mind.

To transform is to change, make over, renew, reconstruct, alter etc. It is like putting on a new shape and figure (metamorphosis); it is a spiritual make over, just as a beautician will prepare or do a make-up for someone for a special photograph or occasion. So believers are not to conform to this world with all its evil and corruption but be transformed by the renewing of their spirit showing new dispositions and inclinations, understanding, enlightenment, the conscience and softened, having rectified thoughts; the will bowed to the will of God, and the affections made spiritual and heavenly.

The man is not what he was before – old things had passed away, all things have become new; he acts from new principles, by new rules and with new designs. You will agree with me that the photographs taken after the beautician had prepared you are entirely different from the ones you've taken casually. The same thing happens after being born again, there must be a definite change. I remember when I became born again, quite a number of things changed in my life. Even my old friends deserted me because they saw the transformation and changes in me. They could not believe what had taken place, a former party conscious fellow, womaniser and drunkard is now cleansed and transformed? **Colossians 3:10 says, "And have**

put on the new self, which is being renewed in knowledge in the image of its Creator. As one takes off dirty clothes and puts on clean ones, so the Christian is called upon to renounce his evil ways and live in accordance with the rules of Christ's kingdom. The putting on of new self or image and the renewing of the mind, is the renewing of the whole man. All the disciples and followers of the LORD Jesus must be nonconformists to this world, we must not fashion ourselves according to the world; we must not conform to the things of the world; they are mutable and the fashion of them is passing away.

PERFECT WILL OF GOD

"Then you will be able to test and approve what God's will is - His good, pleasing and perfect will." Romans 12:2b. The great effect of this renewing which we must labour after is that you may prove what is that good, acceptable and perfect will of God? The will of God is good and acceptable and perfect, three excellent attributes of a law. It is good; it is consonant to the eternal reason of good and evil. The only way to attain His favour at the end is to conform to His will as a rule that is perfect, to which nothing can be added. We also have to test or prove that will of God by knowing it experimentally in conforming to it and by approving things that are excellent. Walking with God in newness of life and spirit demands the renewal of the mind.

ALL THE DISCIPLES AND FOLLOWERS
OF THE LORD JESUS MUST BE
NONCONFORMISTS TO THIS WORLD...

After the spiritual transformation just described has taken place, you will be able to test and appreciate God's will. That which leads to the spiritual and moral growth of the Christian, is pleasing to God not necessarily to us, the will of God may not be pleasing for you but it has to be so after the renewing of your mind. You cannot even add or take away from His will, it is perfect. No improvement can be made on the will of God. Personally, I don't care what human beings say as long as I am in the perfect will of God.

THE PURPOSE OF THE RENEWAL

"That ye put off concerning the former conversation the old man which is corrupt according to the deceitful lusts; And be renewed in the spirit of your mind." – Ephesians 4:22-23.

The mind needs to be renewed in order to restore man to the image and nature of God. This has become necessary due to the effect of the fall which has made the mind corrupt, vain, darkened and totally alienated from the life of God. There is need to put off your old self, that is, the kind of person the Christian used to be, the old life-style of deceitful desires so as to communicate with God. Be effective in our relationship with Him, so as to be made new in the attitude of your minds. Without this renewal, the mind will remain degenerated and depraved and thus, incapable of relating or communing with God.

THE POWER FOR THE RENEWAL

"And the LORD God formed man of the dust of the ground, and breathed into his nostrils the breath of life; and man became a living soul." – Genesis 2:7.

"Create in me a clean heart, O God; and renew a right spirit within me." – Psalm 51:10.

It has been discovered that all efforts of man at personal reformation avails nothing without divine input. The same God who moulded man in the beginning and breathed into him the breath of life must breathe into him again. David asked God to create in him a pure and clean heart, which cannot emerge from what now is (his sinful state) after committing adultery with Bathsheba and which only God can pardon.

This is the power that will transform, transfigure or regenerate the mind to a new one made in the image of the Creator. Titus declared in **Titus 3:5** that it is by the "**washing of regeneration, and renewing of the Holy Ghost.**" Salvation is not achieved by human effort or merit, but comes through God's mercy alone, the new birth is an act of God and it is not achieved by ceremony, but by renewal by the Holy Spirit.

THE PROCESS OF RENEWAL

"For all have sinned and fall short of the glory of God." – Romans 3:23.

What God intended man to be, the glory that man had before the fall, the believer will again have through Christ after recognising their state.

"He who conceals his sins does not prosper, but whoever confesses and renounces them finds mercy." – Proverbs 28:13.

He who hides or covers his sins will suffer physical and psychological pain, but whoever confesses and renounces them finds mercy and forgiveness.

This is a process whereby there is recognition of a sinful state, confession and forsaking of sins; then, believing and receiving Jesus Christ as personal LORD and Saviour. However, as the believer continues to look into the word of God which is the perfect law of liberty, his inner man is renewed day by day and he is able to walk with God. It is possible to be working for the LORD without a renewed mind. The Christian or the Christian worker could be deceived by the progress he is making in the work of the LORD. There is need for a re-examination of the state of our mind and a decision to make our ways right. So I believe God with you that He will renew your mind and give you the grace to keep it renewed in Jesus' Mighty Name.

PRAYER

Father I pray for transformation, complete change in my life, mind, thinking and feelings in Jesus' name.

Father, transform my mind to a new one made in the image of the Creator in Jesus' name.

IT IS POSSIBLE TO BE WORKING FOR THE LORD WITHOUT A RENEWED MIND.

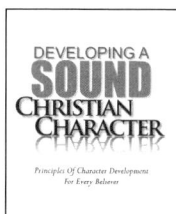

DEVELOPING A
SOUND
CHRISTIAN
CHARACTER

*Principles Of Character Development
For Every Believer*

CHAPTER 4

THE RENEWED THOUGHT

*"Finally, brothers, whatever is true, whatever is noble,
whatever is right, whatever is pure, whatever is lovely,
whatever is admirable-if anything is excellent or
praiseworthy-think about such things."*
PHILIPPIANS 4:8.

Thought is your contemplation, reflection, thinking, meditation etc. For you to develop a sound Christian character, you've got to believe God for a renewal of your thinking process. This Scripture speaks for itself, Paul understood the influence of a person's thinking on his/her life; what a person allows to occupy his mind will sooner or later determine his speech and his action. The combination of virtues (moral worth or excellence, goodness) listed here is sure to produce a wholesome thought pattern, which in turn, results in a life of moral and spiritual excellence. As believers, we need to be careful of what we allow to go through our mind, because our thinking may prompt either positive or negative actions. Moses thought in Exodus 3:3 **"I will go over and see this strange sight-why the bush does not burn up."** Moses' thought prompted him to action when he saw that the bush was on fire but did not burn up.

SPIRITUAL EXCELLENCE

"Avoid every kind of evil." – 1 Thessalonians 5:22.

Every believer is expected to avoid and decline all appearance and every kind of evil. And if you refuse to avoid the appearance of evil, sin, and temptations, you will soon fall into all kinds of evil. With a renewal of thinking it is expected you will have regard to the truth in word engagements, decency and becomingness in behaviour, suited to one's circumstances and condition of life. Fix your thoughts on what is true, honourable and right in all dealings with men, without the impurity or mixture of sin; be honest and be a man and woman of integrity. Also fix your thoughts on what will make you well spoken of, as well as worthy of commendation.

WHY BELIEVERS NEED A RENEWED THOUGHT

"O LORD, you have searched me and you know me. You know when I sit and when I rise; you perceive my thoughts from afar." – Psalms 139:1-2.

God knows every thought, word and deeds, from whom there is no hiding, and He has been privy even to one's formation in the dark concealment of the womb. You need a renewed thought, because God knows you perfectly, far beyond your knowledge of yourself; your every action, your every undertaking and the manner in which you pursue it, even your thoughts before they were fully crystallised and your words before they are uttered. Jesus knows your thought and sees them as well, just as He knew the thoughts of the teachers of the law in Matthew 9:4.

DANGERS OF EVIL THOUGHTS

"The wicked, through the pride of his countenance, will not seek after God: God is not in all his thoughts." – Psalms 10:4. (KJV)

The wicked, through the pride of his countenance, that pride of his heart which appears in his very countenance will not seek God, nor entertain the thoughts of Him. God is not in his thinking and he even has no room for God in his thoughts. God will not be in the thoughts of any projects that have no dependence on Him or has no submission to His will nor aim at His glory.

"The thought of foolishness is sin: and the scorner is an abomination to men." – Proverbs 24:9.

The devising of evil is the thought of foolishness and it is exceedingly sinful, the danger there is that God is not going to be in such thoughts which can lead to an evil action; it is bad to do evil, but it is worse to devise it. Foolish (senseless, unintelligent) thoughts are sinful, so don't allow it, verify it with the word of God as soon as it comes. If you want God to be in your thoughts, think on the things that are true, honest, just, pure, and lovely and of good report, because what you think you will act; either positively or negatively.

DECISION FOR A RENEWED THOUGHT

"Now this is what the LORD Almighty says: "Give careful thought to your ways." – Haggai 1:5.

The decision is yours, you have to give careful thought to your ways, think about what you have done that has provoked God and think about what you will do to testify your repentance, so that God may return in mercy to you. Determine not to entertain the thoughts of evil, adultery and fornication, make a firm decision and you will see God helping and seeing you through.

There is an example of a thought that brought about a miracle in Mark 5:28 **because she thought, "If I just touch his clothes, I will be healed."** This woman had been subject to bleeding for twelve years and had suffered a great deal under the care of many doctors and had spent all she had, yet instead of getting better she got worse. When she heard about Jesus, she came up behind Him in the crowd and touched His cloak, because she had thought about it, her thought brought about her action to touch and her action brought about her healing. I encourage you to make a firm decision today as you are reading this book to think on the things that will bring blessings not only to you but others also. I am not saying that evil or foolish thoughts will not come, but you have a responsibility to cancel and reject it immediately with the Scripture.

PRAYER

Father, I submit my thoughts to you, help me to think on those things that are true, noble, right, pure, lovely and admirable in Jesus Mighty Name.

Father please renew my thoughts and give me the grace and boldness to cancel and reject evil and foolish thoughts as they come in Jesus' mighty name.

YOU NEED A RENEWED THOUGHT,
BECAUSE GOD KNOWS YOU PERFECTLY,
FAR BEYOND YOUR KNOWLEDGE
OF YOURSELF...

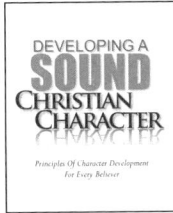

DEVELOPING A
SOUND
CHRISTIAN
CHARACTER

*Principles Of Character Development
For Every Believer*

CHAPTER 5

THE RENEWED CONSCIENCE

"Holding on to faith and a good conscience. Some have rejected these and so shipwrecked their faith."
1 Timothy 1:19.

For you to develop a sound Christian character, you need to believe God to renew and enlighten your conscience. Conscience is a moral sense, a person's sense of what is right and wrong, especially in his own actions or motives, a still small voice. Though this instruction is to Timothy, it should be seen that the purpose of this instruction is that all Christian believers would be filled with love, clear conscience and sincere faith.

HOLDING TO FAITH AND A GOOD CONSCIENCE

We must hold on both to faith and a good conscience, because those that neglect or put away a good conscience will soon shipwreck their faith. It is very important as Christians to live to the directions of a renewed enlightened conscience, and to keep our conscience void of offence toward God and men. Acts 24:16 **"So I strive always to keep my conscience clear before God and man."**

Paul's aim and desire is to have a conscience void (blank, empty, clear, lack) of offence toward God and man, and I believe that this should be the desire of every believer as well. Paul is talking of a conscience not offending; not giving wrong information or flattering him or dealing deceitfully with him or misleading him. We need to have a conscience not corrupt or perverted by any vice or sin, for this will be a means of preserving us in sound faith; we must look to the one as well as the other, for the mystery of faith must be held in a pure conscience. Let us make this intention our constant business as believers and governing principle; let's discipline ourselves and live by the rule to keep peace with our conscience by having a conscience always devoid of offence at all times towards God and man.

So as you read this book, be ambitious like Paul to keep up good terms with your own conscience that it may have no cause either to question the goodness of your spiritual state or to quarrel with you for any particular action. As Pau,l be careful not to offend your conscience, but keep peace with your own conscience, always keep your conscience clear for some people have deliberately violated their conscience; as a result their faith has been shipwrecked.

CORRUPT CONSCIENCE

"To the pure, all things are pure, but to those who are corrupted and do not believe, nothing is pure. In fact, both their minds and consciences are corrupted." – Titus 1:15.

To Christians that are sound in the faith and thereby purified, all things are pure. Meat, drinks and such things that are forbidden under the law (the observances of which some still maintain), in these there is now no such distinction all are pure (lawful and free in their use). However, to those that are defiled and unbelieving nothing is pure; even things that are lawful and good they abuse and turn to sin. They suck poison out of that from which others draw sweetness; their leading faculties - mind and conscience – are defiled and a taint is communicated to all that they do. The thing is that if the conscience is defiled, corruption is communicated to all that you do; corrupt conscience leads to guilty conscience.

> IT IS VERY IMPORTANT AS CHRISTIANS TO LIVE TO THE DIRECTIONS OF A RENEWED ENLIGHTENED CONSCIENCE, AND TO KEEP OUR CONSCIENCE VOID OF OFFENCE TOWARD GOD AND MEN.

1 Timothy 4:1-4, 1-2: "The Spirit clearly says that in later times some will abandon the faith and follow deceiving spirits and things taught by demons. Such teachings come through hypocritical liars, whose consciences have been seared as with a hot iron." Paul is perhaps speaking here of a specific

revelation made to him by the Spirit, that in latter times, some will abandon the faith and follow deceiving spirits and things taught by demons, because the teachings are coming through the teachers that are hypocritical liars, whose consciences are dead and lost to all feelings. These teachers are perfectly lost to the very first principles of virtue and moral honesty, and they cloth themselves with the most barbarous cruelty, under the pretence of promoting the interest of the church, but their consciences are dead that it can no longer say what they are doing is wrong. As believers, we should be very careful about what we pass around the Body of Christ, yours might not be teaching or following wrong teachings, but gossips, backbiting; if you still do this, check your conscience - is it dead or alive?

If you are doing something that is either good or bad, your conscience will tell you, unless you have decided to ignore your conscience.

In John 8:1-11, a woman was caught in adultery and the teachers of the law and the Pharisees brought in the woman, they made her stand before the group and wanted to know what Jesus would say, because the law of Moses commanded them to stone such a woman. However, Jesus said to them, if any one of you is without sin, let him be the first to throw a stone at her, but verse 9 **says, "At this, those who heard began to go away one at a time, the older ones first, until only Jesus was left, with the woman still standing there."**

They began to go away; because they were not "without sin" (v7), the older ones mature in adultery were the first to realise what was involved. They were convicted by their own conscience; like a magistrate in the soul it convicted them.

Teachers of the law and the Pharisees had the wound of conscience; their guilty conscience condemned them, stricken they retired with shame.

CLEAR CONSCIENCE

Clear conscience is a plain, transparent and free conscience, blank of offence towards God and man as it had been earlier mentioned in this chapter. For you to have clear conscience, you must be very cautious that you do not think or speak or do anything amiss against God and man.

2 Corinthians 1:12 says, **"Now this is our boast: Our conscience testifies that we have conducted ourselves in the world, and especially in our relations with you, in the holiness and sincerity that are from God. We have done so not according to worldly wisdom but according to God's grace."** The voice of conscience is the voice of God to a believer and conscience witness more than a thousand witnesses. Paul in defending his trustworthiness against the slanders being spread about him, appeals to the witness of his own conscience and to the Corinthians' firsthand knowledge of his character.

Can your conscience as a believer testify that your conduct in the world, in your relations with non-believers and believers are in holiness and sincerity? Where do you stand? Paul with others consciences testifies concerning their constant course and tenour of life; by this they judged themselves. This blessed apostle, a true Israelite, a man of plain dealing; you would know where to place him always. He was not a man who seemed to be one thing to a person and something else to another; but he was a man of sincerity. If your conscience is clear, void of offence towards God and man, you will rejoice in the testimony of your conscience at all times and in all conditions. Dedicate your conscience to God today, and you will see Him helping you to have a clear and clean conscience.

PRAYER

Father, I submit my conscience to you, cleanse and remove any corruption and defilement in Jesus' mighty name.

Father, in Jesus' name renew and enlighten my conscience, make my conscience clear of offence towards God and man.

THE VOICE OF CONSCIENCE
IS THE VOICE OF GOD TO A BELIEVER

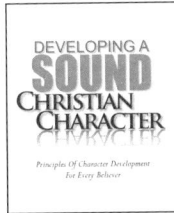

DEVELOPING A
SOUND
CHRISTIAN
CHARACTER
*Principles Of Character Development
For Every Believer*

CHAPTER 6

THE RENEWED LOVE

"If anyone says, "I love God," yet hates his brother, he is a liar. For anyone who does not love his brother, whom he has seen, cannot love God, whom he has not seen."
1 John 4:20.

For you to develop a sound, perfect Christian character, you need to believe God to renew and re-establish your love for God, saints and the sinners. This is a subject, which many Christians are familiar with and think that they know all about, however, the Bible tells us that God is love (**1 John 4:8 says, Whoever does not love does not know God, because God is love**). It is only those who are to some degree like God that truly knows Him, God is love in His essential nature and in all His actions and no one can search out God who is eternal. It is possible that we have only scratched the surface of all we need to know about love. God teaches us more of His love and our duty to love Him and our neighbours through the Bible and our individual life experiences. If you profess to love God and His name, and hate your brother whom you should love for the sake of that God, then you are a liar.

Naturally, you tend to love what is seen rather than what is unseen, your eyes affect your heart; unseen things don't catch the mind and thereby the heart. The incomprehensibleness of God very much arises from His invisibility; the member of Christ has much of God visible in him. How then shall the hater of a visible image of God pretend to love the unseen original, the invisible God Himself! If you say you love God who is unseen, then you should love your Christian brethren created in His image that you see. How can you say you love God when you hate someone created in His image, when you see a monkey, you have seen the image of a monkey, when you see a lion, you have seen the image of a lion, however, when you see a man, you have not seen the image of a man, but the image of God!

Beloved, the whole duty of man is based on two commandments:
a) To love God
b) To love man (**Matthew 22:36-40**), but v40 says, "**All the Law and the Prophets hang on these two commandments.**" That is, the love for God and man.

Friends, this is the sum and substance of all those precepts relating to practical religion which were written in the hearts of men by nature, revived by Moses, backed and enforced by the preaching and the writing of the prophets. All hang upon the law of love; take this away, and all other precepts will fall to the ground and come to nothing. Rituals and ceremonies must give way to these, as must all spiritual gifts, for love is the more excellent way. As you read this book, I want you to understand that this is the spirit of the law, which animates it, the cement of the law, which joins it; and it is the root and spring of all other duties, the compendium of the whole Bible; for the fulfilling of the law is love (**Romans 13:10**) and the end of the law is love, **1 Timothy 1:5.** Our making heaven depends on our success in fulfilling these two major commandments. So you see how important love is for God, for the saints and even for the sinners in developing a sound Christian character.

LOVE FOR GOD

"Love the LORD your God with all your heart and with all your soul and with all your strength." – Deuteronomy 6:5.

Love for God is not just a profession, but a way of life. It entails not just the use of the lips or mouth but of the spirit, soul and body. You have to understand that the love of God and your neighbour is built on the love that the LORD has for His people (**1 John 4:19-21**) and on His identification with them. Such love is to be total, involving your whole being.

The renewed love will be the one that your whole life is focused on pleasing God. Obedience to His commandment in every aspect of life is expected, for without it, life will be meaningless. Our mouths should be full of praise for God; there should be more intimacy, closeness to God that cannot be shattered, a yieldedness that corresponds to a humble heart.

If you profess to love God, there must be constant communion through the priviledge of prayer, the more we do these things, the more we experience the richness and depth of God's love for us. So it is important that you love God above all and then your husband, wife, children, family, career etc. In fact, the love of God should come first, then your family, before we can talk of your business, work or any other thing.

LOVE FOR SAINTS

"A new command I give you: Love one another. As I have loved you, so you must love one another." – John 13:34.

A new command, in a sense it was an old one **Leviticus 19:18 "Do not seek revenge or bear a grudge against one of your people, but love your neighbour as yourself. I am the LORD",** but for Christ's disciples it was new, because it was the mark of their brotherhood, created by Christ's great love for them. As I had loved you, our standard is Christ's love for us. As Christians, we must allow God to renew our love, so that we can love each other compulsorily especially people of the household of faith. It is a commandment that we love one another, the love of God does not exist until we love one another.

A church or group of believers is marked out from another entity by the love of the members for another. **1 Peter 1:22 ... "love one another deeply, from the heart."** He who does not love remains in death, anyone who hates his brother is a murderer **1 John 3:14&15.** If you love a fellow believer, you will do good to them. **Galatians 6:10 says, "Therefore, as we**

have opportunity, let us do good to all people, especially to those who belong to the family of believers." The amount of good you do to believers shows how loving you are towards them.

We love one another by having fellowship, showing good, holy examples of unity and care. You show love also through rebuke and correction while tolerance and trust are some other marks of love among believers. It is a sad reflection on a church if there is no longer trust, we must avoid rumours, backbiting and gossips. Doing these is the surest way of understanding love in a church, so let us love and celebrate one another.

LOVE FOR SINNERS

While Jesus was having dinner at Matthew's house, many tax collectors and "sinners" came and ate with him and his disciples. – MATTHEW 9:10

I believe Jesus was doing this to pass across a message to the people around; He loved the sinners and identified with them, if we don't love sinners or we distance ourselves from them; how then can we win them to Christ? **JOHN 3:16 says "For God so loved the world that he gave his one and only Son, that whosoever believes in him shall not perish, but have eternal life".** God's love of the world (all people on earth) is the great truth that motivates His plan of salvation, if He doesn't love the sinners He wouldn't have sent His one and only Son to die for the world.

Our love for sinners becomes evident by the fervency of our

evangelism. How often do we preach the gospel? Do we invite them to the church? Are we showing love to the sinners by warning them of the judgment to come? How much effort are we putting into praying for them? Do we labour to go out with love to search them out? Sinners are not to be avoided like a trash or refuse, they are to be loved.

Bringing the sinners to Christ, caring for them and showing them love practically are the best ways to love them. I have read several books by one of my favourite author, John Maxwell and one of his quotes I so much cherish is *"People don't care what you know, until they know how you care"*. So care for people and they will go an extra mile for you.

PRAYER

Father, please renew my love for You, so that I can love You with all my heart and with every thing that is within me. Also renew my love so that I can love my fellow saints and sinners that you created in your own image in Jesus' mighty name.

THE AMOUNT OF GOOD YOU
DO TO BELIEVERS SHOWS HOW
LOVING YOU ARE TOWARDS THEM.

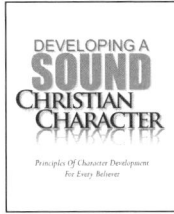

DEVELOPING A
SOUND
CHRISTIAN
CHARACTER

*Principles Of Character Development
For Every Believer*

CHAPTER 7

THE RENEWED TONGUE

*"We all stumble in many ways.
If anyone is never at fault in what he says,
he is a perfect man, able to keep his whole body in check."*
James 3:2.

For you to develop a sound Christian character, you will need to believe God to renew your tongue, since the tongue is so difficult to control, anyone who controls it perfectly gains control of himself in all other areas of life as well. The human tongue can no man tame; it is restless (undisciplined, irreconcilable) evil, full of deadly poison **James 3:8**, for your tongue to be tamed and renewed, it will require great watchfulness, pain and prayers to keep it in due order. James focused more on the whole person and on the destruction of the impure speaker's own life. Also, it is about spreading of sin from your speech to the rest of your life, when your speech is right, your character is right, when your speech is wrong, your character will be wrong. Fellow believers, though the tongue is a little member, it is able to break through all bounds and rules, and spit out its poison on one occasion or the other, notwithstanding the utmost care. If you tongue is faulty then you are at fault.

The Bible says in **Psalm 37:30, "The mouth of the righteous man utters wisdom, and his tongue speaks what is just."** Part of the character of a righteous man is that his mouth speaks wisdom; not only wisely, but he speaks wisdom. His tongue talks not of things idle and impertinent, but of judgement that is, of the word and providence of God and the rules of wisdom for the right ordering of the conversation. The same applied to the women, for out of the abundance of a good heart will the mouth speak that which is good and to the use of edifying.

So be very careful not to spread sin from your speech to the rest of your life, because if you do not discipline and purify your speech, you will not discipline or purify the rest of your life. Let your speech be right so that your character can be right also, refrain from speaking with sarcasm and insults, bless people with your tongue, do not curse or gossip.

> … WHEN YOUR SPEECH IS RIGHT, YOUR CHARACTER IS RIGHT, WHEN YOUR SPEECH IS WRONG, YOUR CHARACTER WILL BE WRONG.

THE SMALL PART

"Likewise the tongue is a small part of the body, but it makes great boasts. Consider what a great forest is set on fire by a small spark." – James 3:5.

As the helm is a very small part of the ship **James 3:4**, so is the tongue a very small part of the body; but the right governing of the helm or rudder will steer and turn the ship as the governor pleases; and a right management of the tongue is, in a great measure, the government of the whole man. The ship is so large but is driven by strong winds; it is steered by a very small rudder wherever the captain want it to go. You see there is great meaning in these wonderful comparisons to show how things of small size may yet be of vast use. And hence we should learn to take more time to study the management of our tongues, because, though they are a little members, they are capable of doing a great deal of good or a great deal of hurt to our life. Therefore we are taught to dread an unruly tongue as one of the greatest and most pernicious evils. It is compared to a little fire placed among a great deal of combustible matter, which soon raises a flame and consumes all before it. Though small there is abundance of sin in the tongue that it may be called a world of evil, there is a great pollution and defilement in sins of the tongue, the whole body is often drawn into sin and guilt by the tongue. Therefore Solomon says **"Do not let your mouth lead you into sin"**. – Ecclesiastes 5:6.

Proverbs 18:21 says, "The tongue has the power of life and death, and those who love it will eat its fruit." The tongue has a blazing power to destroy, there is power of death and life in the tongue and they who mis-use it shall eat the fruit of it for death or life, in other word the tongue can kill or nourish life. The renewed tongue is the one that nourish life, so make up your mind to use your tongue to nourish the life of your husband, wife, children, colleagues, fellow Christians and all, for as you love it you will eat the fruit of it.

THE DECISIVE INFLUENCE OF THE TONGUE

"We all stumble in many ways. If anyone is never at fault in what he says, he is a perfect man, able to keep his whole body in check. When we put bits into the mouths of horses to make them obey us, we can turn the whole animal." – James 3:2-3.

The controlling of your tongue is a decisive matter, influencing the entirety of your life. Our speech is so influential over the rest of our body, so make a decision today as you read this book to control your tongue, if you can control what you say; you can control the rest of what you do as the bits in the mouths of the horses make them obey us in turning the whole animal. Refrain your tongue from evil and deceit, because he whose tongue is deceitful falls into trouble.

The tongue of the righteous is choice silver, but he who holds his tongue is wise. Proverbs 10:20. What the righteous says has great value, so let your tongue influence your whole body in a good and positive way, because our actions and what we say can influence the non-believer for good or for evil.

In James 3:4, the principles were illustrated with two analogies;

the horse's bit and the ship's rudder. Both images have to do with steering, and so refer to the directing of one's whole life, this emphasises the magnitude of the tongue's influence. The tongue has potential for good, speaking godly will help you learn godliness in other ways. If you want purity and Christ likeness to characterise your life, start with your tongue.

THE SPECIFIC DANGERS OF THE TONGUE

"All kinds of animals, birds, reptiles and creatures of the sea are being tamed and have been tamed by man, but no man can tame the tongue. It is a restless evil, full of deadly poison." – James 3:7-8.

Firstly, the tongue spreads evil, it can spread destruction (backbiting, gossips, evil speaking, slanders, lies etc) though they are small and little member of the body **James 3:5.** They are capable of doing a great deal of good or harm. One act of evil starts a destructiveness that spreads beyond the initial act. They can spread sin from your speech to the rest of your life that is why believers should be careful how they use their tongue; if the non believers can not notice a difference in the way you use your tongue it means there is a problem that needs to be urgently looked at.

Secondly **James 3:6,** the tongue is a world of evil or iniquity, there is such an abundance of sin in the tongue that it may be called a world of iniquity, there is a great pollution and defilement in sins of the tongue. It is a vast system of iniquity, it corrupts the whole person; like fire it spreads through time and affects the foundamental direction of one's life. The affairs of mankind and societies are often thrown into confusion or inflamed by the tongues of men. Another thing is that hell has more to do in promoting the fire of the tongue than men are generally aware of. The devil is expressly called a liar, a murderer, an accuser of the brethren; and, whenever our tongues are employed in any of these ways, they are set on fire from hell. So when your tongue is set on fire from hell, then it will be mischievous, producing rage and hatred, and those things which serve the purposes of the devil.

Thirdly, here we are taught how very difficult a thing it is to govern the tongue. All kinds of animals, birds, reptiles and creatures of the sea are being tamed and have been tamed by man, but no man can tame the tongue. Lions and the most savage beasts, as well as horses and camels, and other creatures of great strength have been tamed and governed by men; so do birds, notwithstanding their wildness; even serpents, irrespective of all their venom and all their cunning, have been made harmless and animals in the sea have been taken by men and made serviceable to them. You see these creatures have not been subdued nor tamed by miracles only (as the lions crouched to Daniel, instead of devouring him, and ravens fed Elijah, and a whale carried Jonah through the depths of the sea to dry land), but what is here spoken of is something commonly done, not only hath been tamed, but is being tamed by man, an example will be the zoo that people pay to visit. Yet the tongue is worse than all these creatures and cannot be tamed by the power and art which serves to tame these animals.

Friends, no man can tame the tongue without supernatural grace and assistance. The apostle does not intend to represent it as an impossible task, but as an act that is extremely difficult, which therefore will require great watchfulness, pain and prayer to keep it in due order. It is a restless evil, full of deadly poison. Brute creatures may be kept within certain bounds, they may be managed by certain rules, and even serpents may be so used as not to hurt with their poison; but the tongue is apt to break through all bounds and rules, and to spit out its poison on one occasion or the other, despite the utmost care. So that not only does it need to be watched, guarded and governed just like an unruly beast or a poisonous creature, but much more care and pain will be needful to prevent the mischievous outcomes and effects of the tongue.

THE DECISION TO SPEAK GODLY

"With the tongue we praise our Lord and Father, and with it we curse men, who have been made in God's likeness." – James 3:9.

With the help of God, we've got to decide to speak Godly, because we can't use the same tongue that we use to praise God to curse mankind created in the image of God. Let us decide to keep it from cursing, censuring, and every thing that is evil on all occasions. How absurd is it that those who use their tongues in prayer and praise should ever use them in cursing, slandering, and the like! If we bless God as our father, it should teach us to speak well of, and kindly to all who bear His image. The apostle shows that contrary effects from the same causes are monstrous and cannot be found in nature and therefore not consistent with grace: **v11 "Can both fresh water and salt water flow from the same spring? V12 My brothers, can a fig tree bear olives, ..."** True Christianity will not permit contradictions; and a true child of God can never allow them either in his words or his actions. If we praise God and curse our neighbours, our praise is contradicted. Praising God on Sunday or privately while abusing people with ridicule, insults and attacks through the rest of the week! It cannot be, praising and cursing from the same mouth. The examples from nature **James 3:11-12** are intended to describe situations that never happen e.g. a salt spring does not produce fresh water, the implication is that a true Christian will not make a practice of unchristian speech. **Matthew 12:34** make a decision today to use your tongue well **"For out of the overflow of the heart the mouth speaks"**.

Proverbs 21:23 says, "He who guards his mouth and his tongue keeps himself from calamity." The renewed tongue guards his mouth, allow his speech to be purified and keep the discipline of his or her speech in place. You see it takes discipline to be **"Quick to listen, slow to speak and slow to become angry"** James 1:19. So keep your tongue from calamity. Make up your mind, decide to discipline yourself by purifying your speech, control your tongue, change your speech habits and ask God for the grace needed, for there is no justification for corrupt habit of speech at all to your neighbour, household, colleagues and even to yourself. Repent and you will see God helping you through.

PRAYER

LORD Jesus, I repent in any way that I have used my tongue in an unpurified way and I ask that you will renew my tongue from today.

Father, purify my speech, help me and give me the needed grace to change my speech habits in Jesus' mighty name.

Father, anoint my tongue, so that blessing will be coming out of it in Jesus' mighty name.

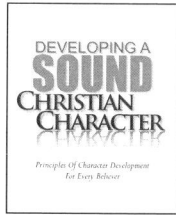

DEVELOPING A
SOUND
CHRISTIAN
CHARACTER

*Principles Of Character Development
For Every Believer*

CHAPTER 8

THE RENEWED WALK

"This I say therefore, and testify in the Lord, that ye henceforth walk not as other Gentiles walk, in the vanity of their mind, Having the understanding darkened, being alienated from the life of God through the ignorance that is in them, because of the blindness of their heart."
Ephesians 4:17-18.

For you to develop a sound Christian character, you need a new walk with God in your calling, career, field, vocation. You will also need a close relationship and fellowship with God to walk with Him, because life without God is intellectually frustrating, useless and meaningless. Gentiles are generally those who are not Israelites, but the Gentiles that have come to the knowledge of the Saviour are different from the unbelieving Gentiles, so we are encouraged not to walk as the unbelieving Gentiles do in the vanity of their mind. For the time to come, because of your calling, you do not live and behave yourself as ignorant and unconverted heathens do. They are wholly guided by an understanding focused on vain things, their idols, worldly possessions and things which are no way profitable to their souls, and which will obscure their expectations. Converted Gentiles must not live as unconverted Gentiles do. Though we live among them, we must not walk like them.

The renewed walk is a close fellowship with God; we should not be like the unregenerate Gentiles out of which regenerated Christians were snatched as brands out of the burning. Verse 18 talks about their understanding being darkened, they were void of all saving knowledge; yes, ignorant of many things concerning God which the light of nature might have taught them. They sat in darkness, and they loved it rather than light, and by their ignorance and blindness of the heart they were alienated from the life of God and preferred to walk in darkness.

The ultimate purpose of spiritual revival is a new walk with God. The unregenerated walk in the vanity of their minds based on deceitful lusts but the renewed mind walks worthy of the calling of the LORD. If we are to live and serve God acceptably, we have no option than to submit our hearts to His spiritual operation so that we can walk in newness of life.

THE PROOF OF SPIRITUAL RENEWAL

"Therefore, since Christ suffered in his body, arm yourselves also with the same attitude, because he who has suffered in his body is done with sin. As a result, he does not live the rest of his earthly life for evil human desires, but rather for

the will of God. For you have spent enough time in the past doing what pagans choose to do–living in debauchery, lust, drunkenness, orgies, carousing and detestable idolatry. They think it strange that you do not plunge with them into the same flood of dissipation, and they heap abuse on you." – 1 Peter 4:1-4.

The evidence of spiritual renewal is a new life and new walk with God; you have to arm yourself so that the sinful desires and practices that once seemed important now will be insignificant as a result of the renewed walk. The proof will be visible to see, because the believer will now rather live for the will of God. The unregenerate Gentiles will think it strange that you do not plunge with them into the same flood of dissipation (disintegration).

This reminds me of the time that I surrendered and gave my life to Christ, my old friends deserted me; they could not believe that I become born again. Why? Because of the kind of life that we used to live together in the past: lust, drunkenness, womanising etc, and they could see the proof of my new walk with God, so they drew back from walking with me. If your old friends cannot see any change in you after salvation, something is wrong somewhere.

A person that has decided to start a new walk with God should not walk in the way of those who do not know God. Just like I did when I became born again, I ceased from walking in my old ways; since I knew that I have been recreated and called to walk in newness of life. **2 Corinthians 5:17 "Therefore, if anyone is in Christ, he is a new creation; the old has gone, the new has come!"** Praise God all things are restored or created new just because you are now united with Christ through faith in Him and commitment to Him; this is the proof of spiritual renewal. It is like someone who has attended a new school or changed to a new course of study, he comes out facing a new direction and mission in life, living a transparent life, the Spirit of God coming against any spirit that wants to interfere with the Grace of God in your life, people around you will feel and see it. This is the proof of Divine renewal.

THE PATTERN OF THE RENEWED WALK

The pattern of the new walk is walking: in the truth, **(3 John 3-4)** in the light, **(1 John 1:5-7 "This is the message we have heard from him and declare to you: God is light; in him there is no darkness at all. If we claim to have fellowship with him yet walk in the darkness, we lie and do not live by the truth. But if we walk in the light, as he is in the light, we have fellowship with one another, and the blood of Jesus, his Son, purifies us from all sin.)"**

Light represents what is good, true and holy, while darkness represents what is evil and false. Walking in darkness and walking in the light are two lifestyles–one characterised by wickedness and errors and the other by holiness and truth. In love **(Ephesians 5:2)** living a life of love, just as Christ loved us and gave Himself, walking in faith **(2 Corinthians 5:7 KJV - "For we walk by faith, not by sight")**, walking in the Spirit **(Galatians 5:16 KJV - "This I say then, Walk in the Spirit, and ye shall not fulfil the lust of the flesh.")**, in submission to the will of God, above reproach, as Christ **(1 John 2:6 walk as Christ walked)**, worthy of the vocation **(Colossians 1:10 walk worthy of the LORD)**, in wisdom **(Ephesians 5:15 walk not as unwise, but as wise)**, according to the perfect example **(Philippians 3:17)** and honestly as children of the day.

THOSE WHO WALKED THE RENEWED WALK

"And Enoch walked with God after he begat Methuselah three hundred years, and begat sons and daughters: And all the days of Enoch were three hundred sixty and five years: And Enoch walked with God: and he was not; for God took him." KJV – Genesis 5:22-24.

If you have walked with someone for a very long time you become a very good friend. Friends there is a difference between walking with God and merely living. Enoch so walked with God for 300 years that He took him away to His presence without experiencing death, you better decide today to walk with God.

"Enoch walked with God", Abraham was called in **Genesis 17:1** by God to **"…walk before me and be thou perfect"**. This was the pattern of the walk of our LORD Jesus whom we are called to walk in His steps. It is this life that enhances ministerial progress, and fruitfulness, thus realising divinely imparted spiritual potentials. **1 Peter 2:21 "To this you were called, because Christ suffered for you, leaving you an example, that you should follow his steps."** Let us follow Christ's supreme example of suffering evil for doing good.

CALL TO DECISION

"Examine yourselves to see whether you are in the faith; test yourselves. Do you not realize that Christ Jesus is in you–unless, of course, you fail the test?" 2 Corinthians 13:5.

Look into your own heart, examine and test yourself, then make a decision today to walk in newness with God. You cannot be a servant of Jesus and be walking as an enemy. If we are to live and serve God acceptably, we have no option than to submit our hearts to this spiritual operation so that we can walk in newness of life.

PRAYER

Search me O LORD if there be any wicked walk take it away, touch and change my life so that I can walk in newness of life with You.

From now on Father help me to walk in truth, light, love, faith, wisdom, in the Spirit, according to the Your perfect will and honestly as a child of light in Jesus' mighty name.

Right now, I submit myself to your spiritual operation so that I can walk in newness of life.

THOUGH WE LIVE AMONG THEM,
WE MUST NOT WALK LIKE THEM.

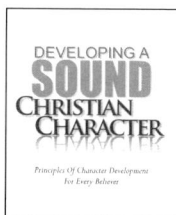

DEVELOPING A
SOUND
CHRISTIAN
CHARACTER

Principles Of Character Development For Every Believer

CHAPTER 9

THE RENEWED VISION

"After the people saw the miraculous sign that Jesus did,
they began to say, "Surely this is the Prophet who
is to come into this world." Jesus, knowing
that they intended to come and make him king by force,
withdrew again to a mountain by himself."
John 6:14-15.

For you to develop a sound, perfect and solid Christian character, you need to believe God to renew, enlarge and stretch your vision; so that you can see beyond now and be spiritually alert. When your vision is renewed you see things in different perspective and you see with your inner or spiritual eyes. The people after they saw the miracle of provision and may be, remembered the food and water God provided through Moses concluded that surely Jesus was a prophet that came into the world. They then wanted to make Him king by force, distracting Him from His vision.

Jesus rejected the world's version of kingship as a temptation of the devil, because He has been destined to be our heavenly King. If you know what the vision for your life is, you will not allow yourself to be distracted thereby allowing the devil to truncate your destiny.

Vision is the faculty of seeing, you need this imaginative insight into the things of God; you also need this kind of foresight and wisdom in planning for your future and your journey's end. Friends, you need to see beyond now and allow the vision (what you see with your spiritual eyes) to condition your life. What is your vision? Is it still the same before you became a believer or has it been renewed? Jesus vision, His foresight is to be the Heavenly King that will rule on the earth and not of any nation. If your vision has been renewed, no one and I say no one will be able to distract you from fulfilling God's intention for your life, because you know what you want and where you are going. His kingdom is not of this world, so friends, don't loose sight of eternal life, don't forfeit it for this earth.

SEEING BEYOND NOW

"All these people were still living by faith when they died. They did not receive the things promised; they only saw them and welcomed them from a distance. And they admitted that they were aliens and strangers on earth. People who say such things show that they were looking for a country of their own. If they had been thinking of the country they had left, they would have had opportunity to return. Instead, they were longing for a better country-a heavenly one. Therefore God is not ashamed to be called their God, for he has prepared a city for them." – Hebrews 11:13-16.

Abraham and other heroes of faith saw beyond their present moment, friends, in your vision lies your future. By faith this heroes saw dimly this heavenly realities and were sure that what they hoped for would ultimately be theirs and as strangers on earth, their true home was in heaven. They were longing for a better country a heavenly one, the New Jerusalem which God has prepared for them. The question now is what are you seeing?

Romans 8:24-25 "For in this hope we were saved. But hope that is seen is no hope at all. Who hopes for what he already has? But if we hope for what we do not have, we wait for it patiently." That's it, hope that is seen is no hope at all, friends you cannot hope for what you already have or seen. Your renewed vision will keep you watching and waiting.

WAITING AND STRAINING FORWARD

"Brothers, I do not consider myself yet to have taken hold of it. But one thing I do: Forgetting what is behind and straining towards what is ahead, I press on towards the goal to win the prize for which God has called me heavenwards in Christ Jesus." – Philippians 3:13-14.

Paul is forgetting what is behind, though not losing all memory of his sinful past, but leaving it behind him as done with and settled. Paul's ultimate aspirations are found not in this life but in heaven, because Christ is there. He focused on this one thing, forgetting the past and looking forward to what lies ahead.

Vision will make you strain towards what is ahead, looking forward to what lies ahead; friends let this be your aspiration. As believers let us focus all our energies on this one thing (vision), straining every nerve, muscle and using every ounce of our strength to win, like Paul let us have the winners' mentality. What Paul is trying to say here I believe is that "my future depend on it, I am running for my life, I pursue the white line, my eyes is fixed on it, I am on to reach the end of the race, to win and receive the supreme and heavenly prize for which God, through Christ Jesus is calling me up".

It is your turn now, how can you develop a sound Christian character without a renewed vision?

PRAYER

Father, renew and stretch my vision, open my spiritual eyes and let me see beyond now in Jesus name.

Father, give me the grace to look forward to what lies ahead, focusing all my energies so as to win the prize in Jesus name.

AS BELIEVERS LET US FOCUS ALL OUR ENERGIES ON THIS ONE THING (VISION), STRAINING EVERY NERVE, MUSCLE AND USING EVERY OUNCE OF OUR STRENGTH TO WIN...

CHAPTER 10

THE RENEWED TEMPLE

"Do you not know that your body is a temple of the Holy Spirit, who is in you, whom you have received from God? You are not your own; you were brought at a price. Therefore honour God with your body."
1 Corinthians 6:19 – 20.

The believer is metaphorically called the temple of God because each has the Father and Son dwelling in him and the Holy Spirit residing therein also (**1 Corinthians 6:19**). Thus each is the headquarters of God on earth. Friends, the renewed temple is yielded up to God, He is jealous of His church and seeks to destroy whoever spiritually, sensually, socially or physically defiles it **1 Corinthians 3:16 "Don't you know that you yourselves are God's temple and that God's Spirit lives in you?"** Believers together are collectively God's temple, so we should be very careful the way we treat and present our personal temple, because if you don't, it will affect every other member in the temple. Don't hurt, corrupt or destroy His temple (v17) for God's temple is sacred, and you are that temple. The renewed temple must be kept Holy for we are His Sanctuary.

Friends, he that is joined to Christ is one spirit, he is yielded up to Him, is consecrated thereby, and set apart for His use, and is hereupon possessed, occupied and inhabited by His Holy Spirit. This is the proper notion of a temple – a place where God dwells and that is sacred to His use, by His own claim and His creation surrender. *Your body is a temple of the Holy Spirit.* For you to develop a sound Christian character, you must value your body as a sacred place where God dwells and should realise that by the Spirit's presence and power you can be helped against such sins as sexual immorality; **"For he who sins sexually sins against his own body"** (**1 Corinthians 6:18**).

Real Christians are of the Holy Ghost. Must he not therefore be God's? So it is plain and the truth that we are not our own, the renewed temples are yielded up to God and possessed by and for God. This is indeed a virtue of a purchase made of us. *You were brought with and at a price.* In short, our bodies were made for God, they were purchased for Him, they are not our own. If we are Christians, indeed, our bodies are yielded to Him, and He inhabits and occupies them by His Spirit, so that our bodies are not our own, but His. And shall we desecrate His temple, defile it, prostitute it and offer it up to the use and services of a harlot or strange woman? Are you indulging in fornication and adultery with your body or abusing it? Horrid sacrilege! This is robbing God in the worst sense. The temple of the Holy Ghost must be kept holy. Our bodies must be kept as His whom they are, fit for His use and residence.

Fellow believer, the renewed temple must spiritually and physically keep their temples holy (**Psalms 93:5 "...holiness adorns your house for endless days, O LORD)"**, for it is not for fortune or fornication (**1 Corinthians 6:13 "...The body is not meant for sexual immorality, but for the Lord, and the Lord for the body)."** By active repentance from dead works, worship and having faith in the LORD Jesus Christ, each sinner becomes a saint whose body becomes a temple of the Godhead. Friends, let us keep our bodies holy.

A HOLY TEMPLE

"But a man who commits adultery lacks judgment; whoever does so destroys himself. Blows and disgrace are his lot, and his shame will never be wiped away; for jealousy arouses a husband's fury, and he will show no mercy when he takes revenge. He will not accept any compensation; he will refuse bribe, however great it is." – Proverbs 6:32-35.

Flee from every moral defilement; each member of our temple should be presented holy unto the LORD. If a man commits adultery, he lacks judgment and destroys himself and if the husband of the lady will not accept any compensation, how much more is our God that expects that the believer keeps his temple holy. The heart, the thoughts and intents must be separated from the world and from every form of idol completely purged from all filthiness of the spirit and of the flesh, perfecting holiness in the fear of the LORD (**2**

Corinthians 7:1 "Since we have these promises, dear friends, let us purify ourselves from everything that contaminates body and spirit, perfecting holiness out of reverence for God)."

The three Old Testament temples, built by Solomon, restored by Zerubbabel and the one built by Herod for 46 years were called various names. Some names are Holiness (**1 Kings 8:10 "When the priests withdrew from the Holy Place, the cloud filled the temple of the LORD).**" Glorious temple (**Isaiah 60:7 "-and I will adorn my glorious temple).**" Magnificent (**Mark 13:1 "As he was leaving the temple, one of his disciples said to him, "Look, Teacher! What massive stones! What magnificent buildings!").** The temples represented the PRESENCE, PURITY and POWER of God. Keep your temple (body) holy onto the LORD.

A HANDSOME TEMPLE

Depart, depart, go out from there! Touch no unclean thing! Come out from it and be pure, you who carry the vessels of the LORD. – ISAIAH 52:11.

The New Testament change from the physical building to human bodies brought with it also the integrity of the human anatomy. It is important that believers keep themselves holy within and without and believe it or not, we are the bible that people read. If a believer's attitude and conduct do not glorify God, this may discourage unbelievers to the message of Christ. However, God placed a great premium on the physical sanctity of the priests and people during worship or sacrifices at the temple. In the New Testament dispensation, our bodies are to glorify God and so we must be sanitarily clean at all times (**Matthew 6:16-17, 17 "But when you fast, put oil on your head and wash your face)"**, since the natural motions of our lives produce mire and dirt. Jews put ashes on their heads when fasting. Putting oil on the head and washing the face were reserved for joyous occasions, but as believers, keep your bodies clean and handsome all the time; that is the renewed temple. As each priest must be clean inspite of the weather condition, men see and smell our outward appearance (**1 Samuel 16:7 "…Man looks at the outward appearance,…"**) and so we must not misrepresent God to others.

A HEAVENLY TEMPLE

"Let the word of Christ dwell in you richly as you teach and admonish one another with all wisdom, and as you sing psalms, hymns and spiritual songs with gratitude in your hearts to God." – Colossians 3:16.

The earthly temple contained the ark of the covenant (**1 KINGS 8:21 I have provided a place there for the ark, in which is the covenant of the LORD that he made with our fathers when he brought them out of Egypt),** while we are filled with the words of Christ. The gospel is the word of Christ, which has come to us as believers and so it must dwell in us or in our house, not as a servant in a family, but as a master, who has a right to prescribe to and direct all under his roof. It must dwell in us, that is, be always available and at hand to us at every time and have its due influence and use. The temple was a place of offering and we are the aroma of Christ, the fragrance of life (**2**

Corinthians 2:15-16) to them who are alive in Christ. Ordained for prayer and worship like Anna the prophetess who never left the temple but worshipped night and day, fasting and praying **(Luke 2:36-37)** we become the people of prayer and praises to God **(Isaiah 43:21 "the people I formed for myself that they may proclaim my praise)."**

So I encourage you to believe God that He will renew your temple (body) so as to live for Him alone and keep the body as His who you are, and fit for His use and residence. Let Christ dwell in you richly, be a heavenly temple by keeping your body holy. Don't do as the people of the world, because you have been bought with a price and you will see God helping you to live a victorious life.

PRAYER

Father, I pray that you will clean and remove any defilement in my body now and help renew your temple (My body) in Jesus' mighty name.

Father, I pray that you will help me to be purged from all filthiness of the spirit and of the flesh, perfecting holiness in the fear of the LORD in Jesus' mighty name.

BY ACTIVE REPENTANCE FROM DEAD WORKS, WORSHIP AND HAVING FAITH IN THE LORD JESUS CHRIST, EACH SINNER BECOMES A SAINT WHOSE BODY BECOMES A TEMPLE OF THE GODHEAD.

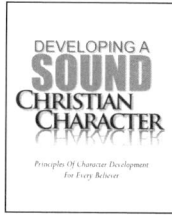

DEVELOPING A
SOUND
CHRISTIAN
CHARACTER

Principles Of Character Development For Every Believer

CHAPTER 11

THE RENEWED BUILDER

"And I answered the king, "If it pleases the king
and if your servant has found favour in his sight,
let him send me to the city in Judah where my fathers
are buried so that I can rebuild it. "
Nehemiah 2:5.

Nehemiah is a historical book. It is a book of restoration and reconstruction and serves as an autobiography of Nehemiah himself. He heard the news about the deplorable condition of Jerusalem; the walls were broken down, the gates burnt with fire, the people were despised and the glory of God was laid in the dust. He wept because he was concerned; he fasted and waited upon God as to what to do. **Nehemiah 1:1-4.** Is there any difference in the church and the world today? The walls of scriptural standard and Godly living in the church are broken down, the restraining gates are burnt with fire, error and falsehood have free access into the body of Christ, the LORD is depending on you today as you are reading this book to rise and be among the builders. God placed the vision of rebuilding Jerusalem in Nehemiah and granted him favour in the eyes of the ruling monarch; he renounced his life of luxury and high position in the palace of Shushan for a life of toil, danger, hardship and opposition from false brethren within and the enemies without. Like Nehemiah be part of the people that will make things happen in your local church, drop every excuse and ignore any opposition from false brethren that are not ready to build, but want to disturb you from building, you will then see yourself developing a sound, unbroken Christian character.

For you to develop a sound Christian character, you need to believe God to renew your attitude towards His work. You see to build is to construct, form, make, establish, start, increase, improve, intensify, etc. Although Jesus said in **Matthew 16:18 "...I will build my church, and the gates of hell shall not prevail against it (KJV)."** I believe that He still needs you as a believer to partner with Him as He builds His church.

Nehemiah took permission to go and rebuild the wall of Jerusalem that had been broken down when the city was invaded and assaulted, because the lack of a city wall meant that the people were defenseless against their enemies. Without a city wall movements cannot be controlled and the enemies or invaders can come in from any angle at any time, night or day. Although Nehemiah was in a foreign land, yet he has the interest of God's people whom God redeemed by His great strength and His mighty hand though they had sinned and failed. **Nehemiah 2:18 "Then I told them of the hand of my God which was good upon me; as also the king's words that he had spoken unto me. And they said, Let us rise up and build. So they strengthened their hands for this good work." (KJV)**

Nehemiah produced the king's commission, told them how readily it was granted and how eager the king was to favour his design, in which he saw the hand of his God upon him. God is ready to help you be a kingdom builder only if you are willing, diligent, and ready like Nehemiah to partner with Him. Nehemiah proposed it to some of the Jews and they came to a resolution, one and all, to concur with him: *Let us rise up and build.*

They were ashamed that they had sat still for so long without as much as attempting this needful work and now resolved to rise up out of their slothfulness and stir up one another. As a renewed believer, you will need to be interested in building with vigour, diligence, and resolution as those that are determined to go through with the building of the broken wall in the society. So break out from procrastination and excuses and help be a builder in your local church. However, the conditions for successful work for God are prayer, planning and perseverance; in building we have to rely on God. **Psalms 127:1 "Unless the LORD builds the house, its builders labour in vain. …"** We need the LORD to help us as we build, because it is Him who provides shelter and security.

BY PRAYER

"When I heard these things, I sat down and wept. For some days I mourned and fasted and prayed before the God of heaven." – Nehemiah 1:4.

For you to be a successful builder, it is important to pray like Nehemiah, because without it you cannot go far; prayer is one of the keys in building the kingdom of God. The desolations and distresses of the church today ought to be a matter of grief to us, however, we live at ease. *He fasted and prayed;* not in public (he had no opportunity of doing that), but before the God of heaven, who sees in secret, and will reward openly. Nehemiah took the right method of fetching in relief for his people and direction for himself in what way to serve them. It is very important for all those who are forming any good designs for the service of the public to take God along with them in prayers uttering all their projects before Him; this is the way to prosper in them.

1 Thessalonians 3:10 "Night and day we pray most earnestly that we may see you again and supply what is lacking in your faith." Not prayers at two set times, but frequent prayers, *most earnestly* translates a strong and unusual Greek compound word that brings out Paul's passionate longing, *what is lacking.* Some of the things lacking were of a practical nature, such as moral and disciplinary matters. Others were doctrinal, such as confusion over Christ's return. So my friend, you see that you cannot start the work of rebuilding without prayer. In Luke 6:12-13 "One of those days Jesus went to a mountainside to pray, and spent the night praying to God. When morning came, he called his disciples to him and chose

twelve of them, whom he also designated apostles." The time has come for an important decision, and so Jesus characteristically spent the night in prayer before the important work of selecting His 12 apostles. Jesus prayed to choose His 12 apostles from among the disciples that followed Him, so you see how important it is to pray before you embark on rebuilding the society.

Spend time first in prayer before God, before you commence in the work of rebuilding.

THROUGH PLANNING

"I went to Jerusalem, and after staying there three days I set out during the night with a few men. I had not told anyone what my God had put in my heart to do for Jerusalem. There were no mounts with me except the one I was riding on." – Nehemiah 2:11-12.

After prayers, you will also need to plan as you get ready to rebuild the walls of scriptural standard and Godly living.

Before the commencement of the work of rebuilding, Nehemiah went out cautiously and discreetly to investigate, fully assess the situation and inspect the condition of the devastation. He arose and set out in the night and viewed the ruins of the walls that he might see what was to be done and in what way they must go about it, whether the old foundation would hold and what there was of the old materials that could be of use. Friends, good work is likely to be done well when it is first properly considered, it is the wisdom of those who are engaged in public business to see with their own eyes a project and not to proceed altogether upon the reports and representation of others and being able to do this without publicity and if possible unobserved. Those that would build up the church's walls must first take notice of the ruins of those walls; those that would know how to amend must enquire what is amiss, what needs reformation, and what may serve as it is. As they say, "He who fais to plan, plans to fail", proper planning, investigation, assessing the walls of your local church base will help in knowing how to get the people converted through personal friendship and mass evangelism.

Without planning, there is no future. We have to plan in building, and as we plan, God will determine and direct our steps.

Proverbs 21:5 "The plans of the diligent lead to profit as surely as haste leads to poverty." When you plan in investigating and inspecting the current condition of the rebuilding that needs to be done, you will surely profit and succeed in the task, but if you refuse to plan then you are planning to fail. So don't lose sight of good planning and insight, hang on to them, they will fill you with life and bring you honor and respect.

PERSEVERANCE

"But when Sanballat the Horonite, Tobiah the Ammonite official and Geshem the Arab heard about it, they mocked and ridicule us. "What is this you are doing?" they asked. "Are you rebelling against the king?" I answered them by

saying, "The God of heaven will give us success. We his servants will start rebuilding, but as for you, you have no share in Jerusalem or any claim or historic right to it.)" – Nehemiah 2:19 – 20.

Nehemiah and his servants persevered despite the opposition from the enemies of progress. Despite the mocking and the ridicule of Nehemiah and his servants, he determined to go ahead in the rebuilding of the wall of Jerusalem; believing that God of heaven will give them success. Enemies like Sanballat and Tobiah may want to distract and disturb you from working for God, the reasons for the opposition were not religious but political, don't give in; be resolute and at the end of the day, you will be a finisher and a winner. A renewed builder will not follow those who are not ready to build or those who are disturbing others. Some of them are as in **2 Timothy 3:5 "having a form of godliness but denying its power. Have nothing to do with them.** They **2 Timothy 3:8 "... oppose the truth - men of depraved minds, who, as far as faith is concerned, are rejected."**

Don't listen to them, go ahead and embark on the work of rebuilding. The fact is that some so called believers are going nowhere, they are busy building their own worldly business and they are disturbing the kingdom builders, if you are serious about kingdom work, don't listen to them; be engaged for the LORD. In fact, one of the reasons of our salvation is to serve God. We are saved to serve! In every congregation, there are 3 sets of people: 1) People that watch things happen. 2) People that cheer when things are happening and 3) People that make things happen. Which group do you belong to?

Nehemiah and his servants were so determined that, "**From that day on, half of my men did the work, while the other half were equipped with spears, shields, bows and amour. The officers posted themselves behind all the people of Judah who were building the wall. Those who carried materials did their work with one hand and held a weapon in the other, and each of the builders wore his sword at his side as he worked. But the man who sounded the trumpet stayed with me." Nehemiah 4:16 – 18.**

Oh! Nehemiah and his men meant business, they did not allow any thing to disturb or stop the work of rebuilding; they stood against the opposition with determination and perseverance and went on with their work. So have a mind to work and stay at it in your local church and in your community, drop every excuse and be part of the work of rebuilding going on there; cooperation brings victory, revival and deliverance.

THE WALLS OF SCRIPTURAL STANDARD AND GODLY LIVING IN THE CHURCH ARE BROKEN DOWN, THE RESTRAINING GATES ARE BURNT WITH FIRE, ERROR AND FALSEHOOD HAVE FREE ACCESS INTO THE BODY OF CHRIST, THE LORD IS DEPENDING ON YOU TODAY AS YOU ARE READING THIS BOOK TO RISE AND BE AMONG THE BUILDERS.

Because of their perseverance Nehemiah and his men finished the walls that begun with God's roots in 52 days. **Nehemiah 6:15.**

"So the wall was completed on the twenty-fifth of Elul, in fifty-two day." The walls that lay in ruins for nearly a century and a half were rebuilt in less than two months once the people were galvanised into action by Nehemiah's leadership. When you persevere in the work of rebuilding, you will not only do well, but also, you will reach your goal. So get involved in the rebuilding work your local church is doing in the community and in no time at all we will reach our corporate goals and be fulfilled.

However as a renewed builder, you've got to be careful how you build on the foundation that is laid. **1 Corinthians 3:10 "By the grace God has given me, I laid a foundation as an expert builder, and someone else is building on it. But each one should be careful how he builds."** That is it! Your work will be shown for what it is, it will be revealed by fire, and the fire will test the quality of each man's work. If what he has built survives, he will receive his reward, if it is burned up, he will suffer loss; he himself will be saved, but only as one escaping through the flames. So friends what are you using in building? Is it gold, silver, costly stones or wood, hay and straw? Remember fire will test the quality of each man's work.

PRAYER

O LORD take all that is in me and use them in building your kingdom, my life, time, talent, energy and money in Jesus' mighty name.

Every spirit of opposition to the work of rebuilding and expansion, I rebuke and destroy in Jesus' mighty name.

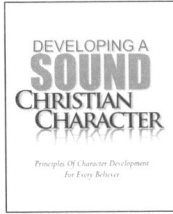

CHAPTER 12

THE RENEWED BELIEVER

*"In the same way, any of you who does
not give up everything cannot be my disciple."*
Luke 14:33.

For you to develop a sound Christian character, you need to believe God to transform you from being a mere believer to a disciple. A disciple is a follower, learner, devotee, student, supporter, etc. In those days and it might still be happening now, Jewish parents will allow their children to live and learn day in day out from the Rabbis. The children lived with the Rabbis so that they can learn, lead and follow the examples of the Rabbis and they can also learn about the things that pertains to the Jews and the laws. For you to be a disciple of Christ, you've got to make up your mind to follow Him every day to the end, *give up everything he has.* The cost of being a disciple according to Jesus is complete surrender to

Him. To be a growing Christian, you must follow Christ's steps; this then produces good works in you. And clearly, only disciples can truly follow Jesus, others are merely believers in Him; for you to be a believer in Christ, is not a big deal, because devils and demons also believes and trembles.

James 2:19 "You believe that there is one God. Good! Even the demons believe that – and shudder." Friends, that is it, it is good that you believe there is only one God but the devil and the demons also believe and trembles, after all God created the devil, but he was sent out of heaven when he rebelled against God. For you to be one step ahead of them; that is the devil and the demons; you need to be a disciple of the LORD Jesus Christ. As a disciple, you would not only master what your teacher Christ knew, but also become like Him in piety (holiness, devotion, duty and faith)

Luke 6:40 "A student is not above his teacher, but everyone who is fully trained will be like his teacher." Every one who is perfect and fully trained will be like the master, every one that would show himself perfect, an established disciple, let him be as his master – dead to the world, and every thing in it, as his Master is. A disciple should live a life of labour and self denial as his Master, and make himself a servant to all; let him stoop and let him toil, and do all the good he can, and then he will be a complete disciple.

In the tradition of the time, Christ's twelve disciples literally lived with him, they traveled with Him, watched all He did and listened to all He said. Friends, for you to be Christ's disciple you've got to follow Him with all your heart, forsaking all, following His steps, learning and listening to Him and serving Him for whom He is. Your life will begin to count for Jesus only when you are transformed from being a mere believer into being a disciple. Friends, discipleship is our opportunity to tap into the infinite resources of God, it is our chance to give our lives to significance rather than mediocrity.

So note that believing God is not a proof that you are justified by faith, because the devil believes and trembles because he cannot stand the power of God and the power in the blood of Jesus, don't rest here move ahead, delight yourself in God, so that you don't live a miserable life. The devil believes but he is far from God, you've got to believe and be close to Him in being a disciple of Jesus Christ. Some so called believers lack self denial, are so selfish of their time, talent and money. You need to totally surrender to Christ before you can be a renewed believer. Let us look at the following three demands of discipleship.

PREFERRING GOD AND CHRIST TO ALL OTHERS

"If anyone comes to me and does not hate his father and mother, his wife and children, his brothers and sisters – yes, even his own life – he cannot be my disciple." – Luke 14:26.

Hates his father. A vivid hyberbole, meaning that someone must love Jesus even more than his immediate family, a man cannot be Christ's disciple if he cannot *hate father, and mother, and his own life.* He must love Christ than anything in the world, and must be willing to part with that which he may and must live as a sacrifice so as to be put in a better capacity of serving God. Abraham parted with his own country and Moses with Pharaoh's court, friends, what is holding you down from preferring Christ than all others? Discipleship is a great price, every good man loves his relations; and yet, if he be a disciple of Christ, he must hate them and must love Christ more than them, as Leah is said to be hated when Rachel was better loved. Not that our relations must be in any degree hated, but our comfort and satisfaction in them must be lost and swallowed up in our love for Christ.

As a renewed believer, when your duty to your parents or family comes in competition with your evident duty to Christ, you must give Christ the preference. Also every man loves his own life, no man hates life; but we cannot be Christ's disciples if we do not love him better than our lives, we've got to love Him more than all even ourselves. You've got to love God as well with all your heart, soul and mind; that is, with your whole being.

Matthew 22:37-38 Jesus replied: "Love the Lord your God with all your heart and with all your soul and with all your mind. This is the first and greatest commandment."

Loving God more than all is the first and greatest commandment, so stop putting God last in your affairs, stop giving excuses on why you cannot serve Him effectively and put Him first above all others, even your family.

TOTAL COMMITMENT

"And anyone who does not carry his cross and follow me cannot be my disciples." – Luke 14:27.

The cross was an instrument of death, but here symbolises the necessity of total commitment – even unto death – on the part of Jesus' disciples. There is need for total devotion, obligation and undertaking to truly be Christ's disciple. A disciple must carry his cross, and come after Christ; he must carry it as if it is a duty, whatever may lie in the way. He must bear it when Christ calls him and in bearing it, he must have an eye to Christ, and seek encouragement from Him, and live in hope of a recompense from Him," **and anyone who does not take his cross and follow me is not worthy of me" Matthew 10:38.** If you cannot take your cross and follow Him, that is it; you are not worthy or qualify to be His disciple.

As a renewed believer, you must deny yourself, putting aside your selfish ambition, shoulder your cross and follow Him. Friends, that is how you can develop a sound Christian character! **"Then Jesus said to his disciples, "If anyone would come after me, he must deny himself and take up his cross and follow me." Matthew 16:24.** Friends, you cannot go after Christ, if you cannot deny yourself to follow Him. No! You've got to deny yourself (forget, ignore, disown, lose sight of yourself and your own interest) then follow Him. As a renewed believer, no one or circumstance should take us away from Christ, let's follow Him throughout our life, let Jesus be in the driver's seat, let Him lead you; just follow with complete and continued obedience, hearing His voice and following Him. **"My sheep listen to my voice; I know them, and they follow me. I give them eternal life, and** they shall never perish; no-one can snatch them out of my hand." John 10:27-28. Jesus knows if you are listening to Him and following Him, if you do; the Shepherd whose sheep's security is in His power will let no one take them from Him. God will keep you because He is greater than all the united forces of men, demons and enemies.

DOING IT DAILY

"Then he said to them all: "If anyone would come after me, he must deny himself and take up his cross daily and follow me." – Luke 9:23.

Take up his cross daily. To follow Jesus requires self-denial, complete dedication and willing obedience. Luke emphasised continued action, daily not weekly, monthly or occasionally, but daily. We must accustom ourselves to all instances of self-denial and patience daily and continually.

Paul counted all other things worthless, he discarded everything else, counting it all as garbage, so that he may have Christ.

Philippians 3:7-8 "But whatever was to my profit I now consider loss for the sake of Christ. What is more, I consider everything a loss compare to the surpassing greatness of knowing Christ Jesus my Lord, for whose sake I have lost all things. I consider them rubbish, that I may gain Christ."

That is it friends! The great reversal in Paul – begun on the road to Damascus, from being self-centered to being centered on Christ. *Knowing Christ Jesus,* not only knowledge of facts, but a knowledge gained through experience that, in its surpassing greatness, transforms the entire person. These verses spell this out, *rubbish*. What Paul possessed as a Christian is not merely preferably or a better alternative; in contrast, his former way of life was worthless and despicable.

So make up your mind not to be a mere believer but a disciple following Christ always.

Make a decision today to develop a sound Christian character and you will see God taking you to greater heights of glory.

PRAYER

LORD Jesus help me to live for you daily preferring you to others and like Paul, to consider everything a loss for the sake of Christ.

Father, I surrender to you in total obedience, help me to love you above all in Jesus mighty name.

SO NOTE THAT BELIEVING GOD IS NOT A PROOF THAT YOU ARE JUSTIFIED BY FAITH, BECAUSE THE DEVIL BELIEVES AND TREMBLES BECAUSE HE CANNOT STAND THE POWER OF GOD AND THE POWER IN THE BLOOD OF JESUS. DON'T REST HERE MOVE AHEAD, DELIGHT YOURSELF IN GOD, SO THAT YOU DON'T LIVE A MISERABLE LIFE.